AF735537

Covid-19 and Wills
The Essential Guide

Covid-19 and Wills
The Essential Guide

Edward Hewitt, LL.B., B.C.L.
Barrister of Lincoln's Inn

Law Brief Publishing

© Edward Hewitt

All rights reserved. No part of this publication may be reproduced, stored in a retrieval system, or transmitted, in any form or by any means, electronic, mechanical, photocopying, recording or otherwise, without the prior permission of the publisher.

Excerpts from judgments and statutes are Crown copyright. Any Crown Copyright material is reproduced with the permission of the Controller of OPSI and the Queen's Printer for Scotland. Some quotations may be licensed under the terms of the Open Government Licence (http://www.nationalarchives.gov.uk/doc/open-government-licence/version/3).

Cover image © iStockphoto.com/DNY59

The information in this book was believed to be correct at the time of writing. All content is for information purposes only and is not intended as legal advice. No liability is accepted by either the publisher or author for any errors or omissions (whether negligent or not) that it may contain. Professional advice should always be obtained before applying any information to particular circumstances.

Published 2020 by Law Brief Publishing, an imprint of Law Brief Publishing Ltd
30 The Parks
Minehead
Somerset
TA24 8BT

www.lawbriefpublishing.com

Paperback: 978-1-913715-09-0

For Gabi, the best thing that

ever happened to me.

CONTENTS

Chapter One	Introduction	1
	1.1 The Covid-19 pandemic, lockdown and consequences for will making	1
	1.2 The purpose of this guide	2
	1.3 Acknowledgments	2
	1.4 Miscellaneous	3
Chapter Two	The Existing Legal Framework	5
	2.1 Overview	5
	2.2 A lot to think about	5
	2.3 Testamentary capacity	6
	2.4 Knowledge and approval	10
	2.5 Undue influence	11
	2.6 Due execution	13
Chapter Three	Difficulties Caused by the Covid-19 Pandemic and Some Ways to Overcome Them	17
	3.1 Introduction	17
	3.2 Taking the client's instructions – steps before the first meeting	17
	3.3 Taking the client's instructions – the first meeting	18
	3.4 Complying with the 'golden rule'	21
	3.5 Drafting the will	23
	3.6 Explaining the draft will and asking the client to check it	23
	3.7 Amendments	24
	3.8 Execution in person	24
	3.9 Execution over a video link	35
	3.10 Receiving the will back from the client	41

Chapter Four Particular Problems 43
4.1 Client self-isolating or shielding at home 43
4.2 Client in hospital 43
4.3 Client in a care home 46

CHAPTER ONE
INTRODUCTION

1.1 The Covid-19 pandemic, lockdown and consequences for will making

In late January 2020 the first cases of Covid-19 infections were reported in the UK. Having encouraged people to stay at home the previous week, on 23rd March 2020 Prime Minister Boris Johnson announced, in effect, a national lockdown.

The Covid-19 pandemic has had a two-pronged impact on will making. On the one hand, the daily reporting in the media of an ever-increasing number of infections and deaths has undoubtedly galvanised people into putting their affairs in order, including by making a will. Many who had previously thought about making a will but had not actually got round to doing anything about it were suddenly spurred into action. Similarly, would-be testators who had started the will making process by giving instructions, but had then lost momentum and put the matter to one side without actually signing a will, were prompted to pick up where they had left off and conclude the process.

On the other hand, the imposition of a national lockdown and social distancing measures designed to slow the spread of the virus has made the mechanics of the will making process much more challenging. Most solicitors' offices across the country have closed, with staff being asked to work from home. This has made meeting in person with the client at the office impossible. Home visits have also become problematic, not least because the clients for whom they would once have been common, i.e. the elderly or infirm, are also among those for whom Covid-19 poses the greatest risk. All of this makes taking instructions from clients, and then explaining the draft will to them to ensure it accords with those instructions, much more difficult. Furthermore, the process of executing a will in the presence of two witnesses who then also both sign it has become a particularly thorny issue, as highlighted by its extensive media coverage.

1.2 The purpose of this guide

Although at the time of writing some of the restrictions are gradually being eased, it seems clear that it is going to take some time before it will be possible to make a will in the way it was before the pandemic. The purpose of this short guide is to consider some of the challenges which the Covid-19 pandemic has created for those in the business of will preparation, and some of the ways in which these might be overcome. The guide assumes some pre-existing familiarity with will preparation, as the basics will not be covered.

1.3 Acknowledgments

I am extremely grateful to the following, who were kind enough to take time out of their busy diaries to share with me some of their thoughts and experiences regarding the challenges created by the Covid-19 pandemic and some of possible ways in which they might be overcome: Charlotte Digby at Freeths, Caroline Miller and Oliver Embley at Wedlake Bell, Natalie Payne at Mackrell.Solicitors and Steven Appleton at Brabners. Needless to say, in the conventional way the responsibility for any error or omission is solely mine.

1.4 Miscellaneous

References to the male singular are used for ease and to avoid a repetitive overuse of "he or she" and "his or her". Unless otherwise stated, reference to a will includes a codicil.

I have attempted to state the law as at 29th July 2020. Given the amount of legislative change brought about by the Covid-19 pandemic, and the speed with which it has been – and continues to be – implemented, it is particularly important to continuously carefully check the very latest legislation and guidance.

CHAPTER TWO
THE EXISTING LEGAL FRAMEWORK

2.1 Overview

This chapter is not intended to be a detailed treatise on the law of wills. Rather, what follows is a summary outline of the legal framework within which wills are made in England and Wales. For a more in-depth analysis, reference should be made to the existing leading works on wills.[1]

2.2 A lot to think about

Reading a judgment in a recent probate claim can be a disquieting experience for the will draftsman. As well as the drafting itself (i.e. the process of choosing words which correctly implement the client's instructions), there are several other aspects on which the draftsman needs to keep an eye to ensure that the final product is in fact a valid will which gives effect to the client's testamentary intentions. The main issues[2] to look out for almost invariably tend to be:

- does the client have testamentary capacity?

---

1 e.g. *Theobald on Wills*, 18th ed.; *Williams on Wills*, 10th ed.; *Williams, Mortimer and Sunnucks: Executors, Administrators and Probate*, 21st ed., *Drafting Trusts and Will Trusts: A Modern Approach*, 14th ed.; *Parker's Will Precedents*, 10th ed.; *Parry and Kerridge: The Law of Succession*, 13th ed.

2 The list is not exhaustive. There will be additional issues for the solicitor to think about if, for example, the client is blind, deaf and/or unable to speak, and/or if the client's command of English is poor.

- does the client know and approve the contents of the will?
- has the client been placed under undue pressure by one or more others into making this will?
- has the will been correctly executed?

Each will be considered in turn.

2.3 Testamentary capacity

The test for testamentary capacity was formulated 150 years ago by Cockburn CJ in *Banks v Goodfellow*[3] as follows:

> *It is essential to the exercise of [the power to make a will] that a testator shall understand the nature of the act and its effects; shall understand the extent of the property of which he is disposing; shall be able to comprehend and appreciate the claims to which he ought to give effect; and, with a view to the latter object, that no disorder of the mind shall poison his affections, pervert his sense of right, or prevent the exercise of his natural faculties—that no insane delusion shall influence his will in disposing of his property and bring about a disposal of it which, if the mind had been sound, would not have been made.*

A series of first instance decisions[4] confirms that the *Banks v Goodfellow* test currently remains the test which the court will apply if the validity of a will is challenged after the testator's death, notwithstanding the enactment of the Mental Capacity Act 2005.

---

3 (1869-70) LR 5 QB 549 at 565.

4 *Scammell v Farmer* [2008] EWHC 1100 (Ch), *Walker v Badmin* [2014] EWHC 71 (Ch) and *James v James* [2018] EWHC 43 (Ch).

In *Perrins v Holland*[5] the following six observations were made on how the *Banks v Goodfellow* test applies in the modern world:

> *First, since the test is a common law test it is capable of being influenced by contemporary attitudes. Second, our general understanding of impaired mental capacity of adults has increased enormously since 1870. Third, we now recognise that an adult with impaired mental capacity is capable of making some decisions for himself, given help. Thus fourth, we recognise that the test of mental capacity is not monolithic, but is tailored to the task in hand: Hoff v Atherton [2005] WTLR 99, 109. Fifth, contemporary attitudes toward adults with impaired capacity are more respectful of adult autonomy. Sixth, even the traditional test must be applied in the context of the particular testator and the particular estate. A testator with a complex estate and many potential beneficiaries may need a greater degree of cognitive capability than one with a simple estate and few claimants.*

Key v Key[6] is an illustration of the application of the *Banks v Goodfellow* test in light of the medical advances made in psychiatry since 1870. The 89-year-old testator was held to have lacked testamentary capacity as a result of the combined effect of his pre-existing cognitive impairment coupled with the severe affective disorder caused by the bereavement at the recent loss of his wife of 65 years.[7]

---

5 [2009] EWHC 1945 (Ch) at [40].

6 [2010] EWHC 408 (Ch).

7 Briggs J (as he then was) explained: "*although neither I nor counsel has found any reported case dealing with the effect of bereavement on testamentary capacity, the Banks v. Goodfellow test must be applied so as to accommodate this, among other factors capable of impairing testamentary capacity, in a way in which, perhaps, the court would have found difficult to recognise in the 19th century*" (at [95]).

The testator must generally have testamentary capacity when he executes the will. The enquiry is time-specific, particularly where the testator's capacity fluctuates, either day by day[8] or even hour by hour. It is suggested that in practice this is frequently overlooked by too many practitioners, who tend to focus more on the client's capacity at the meeting during which instructions are given, rather than at the subsequent meeting during which the will is executed. This can result in the contemporaneous evidence of the latter – which is usually the draftsman's attendance note – being much scanter that that of the former. This can be problematic in the event of a subsequent validity challenge, particularly if the testator's capacity fluctuates or is declining and if there is a significant time gap between the two meetings.

It is right to add that even if the testator lacked testamentary capacity when he executed the will, the will might nonetheless be valid if the so-called 'rule in *Parker v Felgate*' is engaged.[9] The 'rule' was explained as follows by Moore-Bick LJ in *Perrins v Holland*:[10]

> *Where the testator loses some of his faculties between giving instructions and executing the will, however, the position is different. One must then ask (i) whether at the time he gave the instructions he had the ability to understand and give proper consideration to the various matters which are called for, that is, whether he had testamentary capacity, (ii) whether the document gives effect to his instructions, (iii) whether those instructions continued to reflect his intentions and (iv) whether at the time he*

---

8 See e.g. *Cowderoy v Cranfield* [2011] EWHC 1616 (Ch), where Morgan J accepted the evidence that the testatrix had "*good days and bad days*", principally as a result of the combined effect of her medication and the consumption of alcohol (at [144]).

9 *Parker v Felgate* (1883) 8 PD 171. The existence of the 'rule' was more recently confirmed by the Court of Appeal in *Perrins v Holland* [2010] EWCA Civ 840.

10 [2010] EWCA Civ 840 at [55].

> *executed the will he knew what he was doing and thus had sufficient mental capacity to carry out the juristic act which that involves. If all those questions can be answered in the affirmative, one can be satisfied that the will accurately reflects the deceased's intentions formed at a time when he was capable of making fully informed decisions.*

However, from the draftsman's perspective, having to rely on the rule in *Parker v Felgate* is obviously unsatisfactory. Instead, care should be taken to ensure that the contemporaneous evidence of the testator's capacity at both the execution meeting and the earlier meeting at which instructions are given is as clear and as comprehensive as possible.

The draftsman should also bear in mind the so-called 'golden rule' formulated by Templeman J (as he then was) in *Kenward v Adams*[11] and *Re Simpson.*[12] In the latter, Templeman J explained:

> *In the case of an aged testator or a testator who has suffered a serious illness, there is one golden rule which should always be observed, however straightforward matters may appear and however difficult or tactless it may be to suggest that precautions be taken: the making of a will by such a testator ought to be witnessed or approved by a medical practitioner who satisfied himself of the capacity and understanding of the testator, and records and preserves his examination and finding.*
>
> *There are other precautions which should be taken. If the testator has made an earlier will this should be considered by the legal and medical advisers of the testator, and if appropriate, discussed with the testator. The instructions of the testator should be taken in the*

11 The Times, November 29, 1975.

12 (1977) 121 Sol Jo 224; (1977) 127 NLJ 487; 1977] CLY 3181.

absence of anyone who may stand to benefit, or who may have influence over the testator. These are not counsels of perfection. If proper precautions are not taken injustice may result or be imagined and great expense and misery may be unnecessarily caused.

2.4 Knowledge and approval

The court's enquiry into whether the testator knew and approved the contents of his will used to involve two stages. First, the court would ask whether the circumstances were such as to 'excite suspicion' on the part of the court. If so, the burden would be on the propounder of the will to establish that the testator knew and approved the contents of the will (and thereby dispel the court's suspicion). On the other hand, if the circumstances did not 'excite suspicion', then the court presumed knowledge and approval in the case of a will which had been duly executed by a testator who had testamentary capacity.[13]

In recent cases there has been a tendency to abandon this approach and to focus instead on the single question whether the testator "*appreciated what was in the will when [he] signed it*";[14] or, to put it another way, whether he "*understood what he was doing and its effect*".[15]

13 See e.g. *Cowderoy v Cranfield* [2011] EWHC 1616 (Ch) at [139].

14 *Gill v Woodall* [2010] EWCA Civ 1430 at [64].

15 See e.g. *Hoff v Atherton* [2004] EWCA Civ 1554 at [64], *Cowderoy v Cranfield* [2011] EWHC 1616 (Ch) at [139], *Wharton v Bancroft* [2011] EWHC 3250 (Ch) at [28(a)], *Schrader v Schrader* [2013] EWHC 466 (Ch) at [86]-[87] and *Burns v Burns* [2016] EWCA Civ 37 at [56].

If the will was properly executed after being prepared by a solicitor and read over to or by the testator, a very strong presumption arises that the will represents the testator's intentions.[16]

2.5 Undue influence

It is notoriously difficult to successfully challenge a will on the basis that it was procured by undue influence. This is primarily because, unlike in relation to lifetime transactions,[17] the challenging party must actually prove undue influence without the benefit of any presumption. The classic modern restatement is that given by Lewison J (as he then was) in *Re Edwards*:[18]

> *i) In a case of a testamentary disposition of assets, unlike a lifetime disposition, there is no presumption of undue influence;*
>
> *ii) Whether undue influence has procured the execution of a will is therefore a question of fact;*
>
> *iii) The burden of proving it lies on the person who asserts it. It is not enough to prove that the facts are consistent with the hypothesis of undue influence. What must be shown is that the facts are inconsistent with any other hypothesis. In the modern law this is, perhaps no more than a reminder of the high burden, even on the civil standard, that a claimant bears in proving undue influence as vitiating a testamentary disposition;*

---

16 See e.g. *Gill v Woodall* [2010] EWCA Civ 1430 at [14]-[15].

17 As to which see e.g. *Royal Bank of Scotland plc v Etridge (No.2)* [2001] UKHL 44 and *Birmingham City Council v Beech* [2014] EWCA Civ 830 at [58]-[63].

18 [2007] EWHC 1119 (Ch) at [47].

iv) In this context undue influence means influence exercised either by coercion, in the sense that the testator's will must be overborne, or by fraud.

v) Coercion is pressure that overpowers the volition without convincing the testator's judgment. It is to be distinguished from mere persuasion, appeals to ties of affection or pity for future destitution, all of which are legitimate. Pressure which causes a testator to succumb for the sake of a quiet life, if carried to an extent that overbears the testator's free judgment discretion or wishes, is enough to amount to coercion in this sense;

vi) The physical and mental strength of the testator are relevant factors in determining how much pressure is necessary in order to overbear the will. The will of a weak and ill person may be more easily overborne than that of a hale and hearty one. As was said in one case simply to talk to a weak and feeble testator may so fatigue the brain that a sick person may be induced for quietness' sake to do anything. A "drip drip" approach may be highly effective in sapping the will;

vii) There is a separate ground for avoiding a testamentary disposition on the ground of fraud. The shorthand used to refer to this species of fraud is "fraudulent calumny". The basic idea is that if A poisons the testator's mind against B, who would otherwise be a natural beneficiary of the testator's bounty, by casting dishonest aspersions on his character, then the will is liable to be set aside;

viii) The essence of fraudulent calumny is that the person alleged to have been poisoning the testator's mind must either know that the aspersions are false or not care whether they are true or false. In my judgment if a person believes that he is telling the truth about a potential beneficiary then even if what he tells the testator is objectively untrue, the will is not liable to be set aside on that ground alone;

ix) The question is not whether the court considers that the testator's testamentary disposition is fair because, subject to statutory powers of intervention, a testator may dispose of his estate as he wishes. The question, in the end, is whether in making his dispositions, the testator has acted as a free agent.

2.6 Due execution

Save for wills made in certain limited exceptional circumstances,[19] in order to be formally valid as a matter of English law a will must comply with section 9 of the Wills Act 1837, which provides:

9. Signing and attestation of wills.

No will shall be valid unless—

(a) it is in writing, and signed by the testator, or by some other person in his presence and by his direction; and

(b) it appears that the testator intended by his signature to give effect to the will; and

(c) the signature is made or acknowledged by the testator in the presence of two or more witnesses present at the same time; and

19 viz. by soldiers "*in actual military service*" and by mariners or seamen "*being at sea*" (section 11 of the Wills Act 1837) and by members of the naval or marine forces "*not only when […] at sea but also when […] so circumstanced that if [they] were a soldier [they] would be in actual military service*" within the meaning of section 11: section 2 of the Wills (Soldiers and Sailors) Act 1918.

(d) each witness either—

(i) attests and signs the will; or

(ii) acknowledges his signature,

in the presence of the testator (but not necessarily in the presence of any other witness),

but no form of attestation shall be necessary.

The need for two witnesses to witness the testator sign his will has proved particularly problematic – and controversial – during the Covid-19 pandemic, which has made it unusually difficult for three people to get together in close proximity. On 25th July 2020 the government announced that wills should continue to be executed in the conventional way, albeit in a way which complies with the latest government advice on, in particular, social distancing. However, the government also announced that legislation will be enacted in September 2020 which will make it clear that the two witnesses can be 'present' within the meaning of section 9 even though they are present over a video link, rather than physically.[20] The change is intended to apply retrospectively from 31st January 2020 and is intended as a temporary measure which will be brought to an end when the pandemic is over. It is discussed in more detail at 3.9.

20 https://www.gov.uk/government/news/video-witnessed-wills-to-be-made-legal-during-coronavirus-pandemic (accessed 29th July 2020).

It is also important to bear in mind section 15 of the Wills Act 1837,[21] which invalidates any gift in a will made to an attesting witness or to their spouse[22] or civil partner.[23]

Section 28(4) of the Trustee Act 2000 makes it clear that payments to a trustee or personal representative[24] in respect of services pursuant to a charging clause in a will "*are to be treated as remuneration for services (and not as a gift)*" for the purposes of section 15 of the Wills Act 1837. Therefore a solicitor can safely act as a witness without thereby jeopardising his right to remuneration pursuant to a charging clause if he is also appointed executor.[25] However, any gift

---

21 *15. Gifts to an attesting witness to be void.*
If any person shall attest the execution of any will to whom or to whose wife or husband any beneficial devise, legacy, estate, interest, gift, or appointment, of or affecting any real or personal estate (other than and except charges and directions for the payment of any debt or debts), shall be thereby given or made, such devise, legacy, estate, interest, gift, or appointment shall, so far only as concerns such person attesting the execution of such will, or the wife or husband of such person, or any person claiming under such person or wife or husband, be utterly null and void, and such person so attesting shall be admitted as a witness to prove the execution of such will, or to prove the validity or invalidity thereof, notwithstanding such devise, legacy, estate, interest, gift, or appointment mentioned in such will.

22 Including same sex spouse: paragraph 1 of Schedule 3 to the Marriage (Same Sex Couples) Act 2013.

23 Paragraph 3 of Schedule 4 to the Civil Partnership Act 2004.

24 Section 35 makes it clear that section 28(4) applies to personal representatives as well as trustees, and section 39(1) defines "*personal representatives*" by reference to the definition in the Trustee Act 1925, viz. "*the executor, original or by representation, or administrator for the time being of a deceased person*" (section 68(9) of the Trustee Act 1925).

25 Note that the solicitor is required to ensure that the client understands that he is not required to appoint the solicitor as an executor: see Solicitors Regulation Authority Guidance "*Drafting and preparation of wills*" updated on 25th November 2019 and available here: https://www.sra.org.uk/solicitors/guidance/ethics-guidance/guidance-on-the-drafting-and-preparation-of-wills/ (accessed 29th July 2020); Law Society practice note "*Appointment of a professional executor*" updated

to the solicitor who acts as a witness will be invalidated by section 15 of the Wills Act 1837. In any event, particular care must be taken about acting at all where the testator proposes to make a significant gift to the draftsman, his family or colleagues.[26]

on 2nd December 2019 and available here: https://www.lawsociety.org.uk/support-services/advice/practice-notes/appointment-of-a-professional-executor/ (accessed 29th July 2020).

26 See Solicitors Regulation Authority Guidance "*Drafting and preparation of wills*" (above); Law Society practice note "*Preparing a will when your client is leaving a gift for you, your family or colleagues*" updated on 16th December 2019 and available here: https://www.lawsociety.org.uk/support-services/advice/practice-notes/preparing-wills-when-your-client-is-leaving-a-gift-for-you-your-family-or-colleague/ (accessed 29th July 2020).

CHAPTER THREE
DIFFICULTIES CAUSED BY THE COVID-19 PANDEMIC AND SOME WAYS TO OVERCOME THEM

3.1 Introduction

Will preparation is an involved process even in normal times. As the summary of the legal framework outlined in chapter 2 shows, there is a lot for the solicitor to think about and do. The Covid-19 pandemic has made the solicitor's job even harder.

This chapter will consider some of the additional difficulties created by the pandemic, and some possible ways to overcome them. The chapter assumes some pre-existing familiarity with will preparation, as the basics will not be covered. Needless to say, solicitors will ultimately have to exercise their own judgment depending on all of the particular circumstances they are faced with.

3.2 Taking the client's instructions – steps before the first meeting

Even before the pandemic, some firms of solicitors had adopted the practice of sending clients pro forma will questionnaires, which they asked clients to complete in advance of the first meeting and either return in advance of that meeting, or bring along with them to the meeting. Given the difficulties in holding face-to-face meetings (considered below), asking the client to complete and return a will questionnaire in advance of the first meeting can be a particularly useful exercise during the pandemic. Doing so is likely to arm the solicitor with information in advance of that first meeting, the logistics of which may be less than ideal. It will also provide the solicitor with additional documentary evidence of the client's instructions, which the solicitor can then refer back to when the time comes to actually draft the will.

In most cases, it should be possible to send the questionnaire to the client by email, perhaps as an editable Word document attachment, and ask the client to complete it on a computer or tablet and email it back. If the firm has the necessary facilities, it may also be possible to ask the client to complete the questionnaire online through a secure area or portal on the firm's website. In cases where electronic means are not feasible, a hard copy of the questionnaire can be sent in the post with a self-addressed stamped envelope. In such cases it is worth checking in advance whether it will actually be possible for the client to post the questionnaire back to the solicitor, and otherwise arrange for some other means for the questionnaire to be returned.

The contents of the questionnaire – particularly any instructions relating to dispositive provisions – will of course have to be carefully checked with the client to ensure that they do in fact represent the client's wishes, and not those of someone who may have assisted the client with completing the questionnaire.

3.3 Taking the client's instructions – the first meeting

In normal times, will instructions are usually taken from the testator during a meeting in person (and sometimes more than one), which is generally held either at the solicitor's office or at the client's home (particularly in the case of elderly or infirm testators). The pandemic and lockdown have of course made all of this much more difficult. Most solicitors' offices closed and staff were asked to work from home. Restrictions against travel and social distancing measures effectively prohibited most face-to-face meetings between solicitors and their clients, whether at the solicitor's office or at the client's home. Even as those restrictions and measures are eased and offices gradually reopen, the former way of conducting meetings seems unlikely to return as the norm for some time.

In the main, face-to-face meetings have been replaced by meetings by video link. The pandemic has seen an explosion in the use of video link software such as Zoom, Microsoft Teams, Cisco Webex, WhatsApp Video and FaceTime. Each of these has its pros and cons, although anecdotal evidence suggests that Zoom has proved a very popular choice, primarily because of its ease of use for clients who might not be very technologically inclined.

Conducting a client meeting by video link requires some steps to be taken in addition to those which would in any event be taken at a face-to-face meeting (such as ensuring that the client has testamentary capacity, that no undue influence is being exerted, that significant departures from previous wills are explained). These additional steps are likely to include:

- Ensuring that the client has access to any necessary software and a stable enough internet connection to enable the meeting to run clearly and smoothly.

- Scheduling the meeting through the relevant software.

- Ensuring that the client receives a link to the scheduled meeting.

- Checking at the outset of the meeting that the client is alone, or at least has some privacy. This is particularly important where the circumstances are such as to alert the solicitor to a risk that the intended new will is likely to be controversial – for example, where the client is self-isolating with one of his adult children and intends to make a will leaving his whole estate to that child, excluding his two other children. It is also important to try to ensure that nobody off camera is prompting answers to a client who is suffering from confusion or memory loss, as this might conceal the fact that the client may not have testamentary capacity. In the same way as one would ordinarily ask family members or others accompanying the client to the office to wait outside the meeting room during a face-to-face meeting, it is suggested that it is explained to the client that they should be in a room on their own for the duration of the video link meeting if possible. To achieve this, it may be worth also ensuring in advance of the meeting that the client is sufficiently familiar with the video link software to be able to use it on his own, possibly by sending some guidance in advance. It may even be worth asking the client to show the solicitor his surroundings by providing a 'virtual tour' over the video link.

- Deciding whether to record the meeting and, if so, obtaining the client's express consent to do so at the outset of the meeting. A potential advantage video link meetings have over face-to-face ones is that many of the video link software options enable meetings to be recorded at the click of a button. The recording can then be saved and stored as part of the (electronic) will file. This could be both useful to consult again when drafting the will, and also as evidence to store against a possible subsequent validity challenge. Any recording will contain sensitive confidential client information and must therefore be protected accordingly. An article on the Law Society's website provides some further guidance on security issues surrounding video conferencing.[1] The

---

1 "Coronavirus (COVID-19): How to video conference safely" https://www.lawsociety.org.uk/topics/coronavirus/coronavirus-covid-19-how-

Information Commissioner's Office has also published an online information hub containing guidance on data protection during the pandemic.[2]

Just like in normal times, it is crucial for the solicitor to make a detailed, comprehensive, and contemporaneous attendance note of the meeting. It may be that a recording of the virtual meeting will serve as the best type of attendance note, but until the profession gets comfortable with this idea, it seems likely that to err on the side of caution the solicitor should keep both any recording and an 'old fashioned' attendance note.

It seems likely that video link meetings will remain a common feature of the will making process for some time. Clients who have made use of video link facilities during the pandemic will have discovered their convenience and become used to them. For as long as Covid-19 remains a risk, having a meeting over a video link rather than in person will probably seem like an obvious step to reduce the risk of infection for both clients and solicitors.

3.4 Complying with the 'golden rule'

In many cases, the solicitor will have no doubt that the client has testamentary capacity. Conversely, in some cases it might be so clear to the solicitor that the client lacks testamentary capacity that the solicitor will have no choice but to refuse to accept instructions. The more difficult cases are of course those that fall between these two extremes.

---

to-video-conference-safely (accessed 29th July 2020).

2 https://ico.org.uk/global/data-protection-and-coronavirus-information-hub/ (accessed 29th July 2020).

If the client is elderly or infirm, or if it is otherwise thought that the will is likely to be controversial and might subsequently be challenged on the ground that the client lacked testamentary capacity, it will usually be sensible for the solicitor to obtain – or at least try to obtain – contemporaneous medical evidence confirming that the client does have testamentary capacity, and to ask the medical practitioner who provides such evidence to act as one of the witnesses, in accordance with the so-called 'golden rule'.[3]

Even before the pandemic, many solicitors struggled to find a suitably qualified medical practitioner who is both willing and able to perform this task. Many generalist GPs tend to indicate that they do not consider themselves to be suitably qualified to assess testamentary capacity. Others are under such pressures of work that they are unable to arrange a consultation with the client for several weeks, or even months. This creates real practical difficulties for the solicitor, given that the cases in which contemporaneous medical evidence is most likely to be important (i.e. where the client is very elderly and/or suffering from a debilitating illness) are also those in which the will-making process needs to be completed as quickly as possible because of the risk that the testator might otherwise die before the will is executed.[4]

One might expect these practical difficulties to have been exacerbated by the pandemic. However, some anecdotal evidence suggests that because many medical practitioners have also had to switch to working remotely, and thus to having patient consultations electronically by video link, it might in fact (somewhat counterintuitively) be easier and quicker to get a medical assessment as to the client's

---

3 See 2.3.

4 For an example of this headache, see the professional negligence case of *Feltham v Freer Bouskell* [2013] EWHC 1952 (Ch).

capacity in Covid-19 times. Arranging for the medical practitioner to witness the will is, however, likely to be much more difficult, if not altogether impossible.

3.5 Drafting the will

When it comes to actually drafting the will, the main challenge the pandemic is likely to create is a reduced access to suitable precedents, particularly if these are kept in hard copy in a library at the office, which may be closed and out of bounds. The main online legal databases – Westlaw and LexisNexis – have a number of helpful precedent books which those working from home can access online (by paying for a subscription).

3.6 Explaining the draft will and asking the client to check it

In non-Covid times, it is common for the solicitor to send the client a draft will under cover of an explanatory letter which explains each clause in layman's terms, so that the client can check the draft to ensure it accords with his instructions before an engrossment is produced. This is often done by email or, if the client does not have email access, by post. If done by email, it is preferable to send both the letter and the draft will as non-editable PDF documents, perhaps with the draft will clearly watermarked 'DRAFT', rather than as a Word document which the client might try to edit himself and then print off and sign.

It is suggested that this important step should also be taken during the pandemic. Email is obviously the preferable option, but post can be used as a fallback if email is not available.

3.7 Amendments

On reviewing the draft will, the client may decide he wants to make amendments to it, either to correct errors (such as the incorrect spelling of one of the beneficiaries' names or addresses) or perhaps because he has changed his mind about some of the gifts made by the draft will. In all cases a clear contemporaneous record of the client's instructions in relation to any amendments should be kept. An email from the client requesting the amendments can speak for itself, although some thought should be given to whether it is appropriate in the particular circumstances to double-check that the email was in fact sent by the client and contains his instructions (and was not, for example, sent by a third party who might have access to the client's email account). A detailed, comprehensive and contemporaneous attendance note should be kept of all telephone calls with the client during which instructions are given. If the amendments are particularly significant and/or surprising in the circumstances, it may be worth trying to arrange a further video link meeting with the client during which these can be discussed in detail.

3.8 Execution in person

The rules governing the way in which a will must be executed in order to be valid, and whether they should be relaxed during the pandemic, have become topics of great controversy as a result of Covid-19. The issue which has proved particularly controversial is whether it is possible – and whether it should be possible – to validly execute a will in circumstances in which the testator and the two witnesses are 'present' virtually over a video link to which they have connected from different geographical locations, rather than all being physically present in person in the same place. This aspect is considered further in the next section. This section will consider the impact the pandemic has had on 'traditional' execution – i.e. on execution involving the testator and two witnesses who are all physically present in the same geographical location.

The rules governing execution are contained in section 9 of the Wills Act 1837, which provides:

> *9. Signing and attestation of wills.*
>
> *No will shall be valid unless—*
>
> > *(a) it is in writing, and signed by the testator, or by some other person in his presence and by his direction; and*
> >
> > *(b) it appears that the testator intended by his signature to give effect to the will; and*
> >
> > *(c) the signature is made or acknowledged by the testator in the presence of two or more witnesses present at the same time; and*
> >
> > *(d) each witness either—*
> >
> > > *(i) attests and signs the will; or*
> > >
> > > *(ii) acknowledges his signature,*
> >
> > *in the presence of the testator (but not necessarily in the presence of any other witness),*
> >
> > *but no form of attestation shall be necessary.*

The section therefore allows for several alternative execution processes, each of which will result in a validly executed will:

(a) The testator signs the will in the presence of two witnesses who are present at the same time and in the same place, and each of whom also signs the will in the presence of the testator (but not necessarily in the presence of the other witness).

(b) The testator signs the will while alone, and then acknowledges his signature in the presence of two witnesses who are present at the same time and in the same place, and each of whom also signs the will in the presence of the testator (but not necessarily in the presence of the other witness).

(c) Someone signs the will on behalf of the testator in the testator's presence and at his (express)[5] direction, and also in the presence of two witnesses who are present at the same time and in the same place, and each of whom also signs the will in the presence of the testator (but not necessarily in the presence of the other witness).

(d) Someone signs the will on behalf of the testator in the testator's presence and at his (express) direction, but not in the presence of any witnesses, and the testator subsequently acknowledges the signature in the presence of two witnesses who are present at the same time and in the same place, and each of whom also signs the will in the presence of the testator (but not necessarily in the presence of the other witness).

(e) The testator signs the will in the presence of two witnesses who are present at the same time and in the same place; each of the witnesses signs the will alone and then acknowledges their signature in the presence of the testator (but not necessarily in the presence of the other witness).

---

5 See *Barrett v Bem* [2012] EWCA Civ 52.

(f) The testator signs the will while alone, and then acknowledges his signature in the presence of two witnesses who are present at the same time and in the same place; each of the witnesses signs the will alone and then acknowledges their signature in the presence of the testator (but not necessarily in the presence of the other witness).

(g) Someone signs the will on behalf of the testator in the testator's presence and at his (express) direction, and also in the presence of two witnesses who are present at the same time and in the same place; each of the witnesses signs the will alone and then acknowledges their signature in the presence of the testator (but not necessarily in the presence of the other witness).

(h) Someone signs the will on behalf of the testator in the testator's presence and at his (express) direction, but not in the presence of any witnesses, and the testator subsequently acknowledges the signature in the presence of two witnesses who are present at the same time and in the same place; each of the witnesses signs the will alone and then acknowledges their signature in the presence of the testator (but not necessarily in the presence of the other witness).

In non-Covid times, a professionally prepared will would usually be executed at a further meeting arranged with the solicitor, either at the solicitor's office or at the client's home. Often the solicitor would act as one of the two witnesses, and another employee of the firm (such as a legal secretary or a trainee solicitor) would act as the second witness. The process adopted in the vast majority of cases would be (a) above. Arranging execution in this way has the advantage of addressing several matters at the same time:

- It makes it easy to ensure that the formal requirements imposed by section 9 are complied with. All solicitors involved in will preparation are familiar – or at least should be familiar! – with the requirements imposed by section 9. If the client is in the solicitor's office or at home meeting the solicitor and another employee of the firm in person, it is usually fairly straightforward to ensure that all three individuals are present at the same time – normally sitting round the same table – when the client signs the will while the two professionals watch him do so. Once the will has been signed by the client, it is then also straightforward for it to be passed to each of the two professionals who in turn also sign while all three individuals are still present.

- It is also a convenient way of making sure that section 15 of the Wills Act 1837 does not accidentally invalidate any gift made by the will. This will happen to any gift in the will made to an attesting witness or to their spouse[6] or civil partner.[7] Neither professional will usually be the intended beneficiary of a gift under the will,[8] and this is therefore a safer route than asking family members or friends to act as witnesses.

- The solicitor will have the opportunity to read over and explain the will to the client clause by clause one more time to ensure that all details are correct and that the will accurately implements the client's testamentary wishes. This is an important exercise, because if correctly carried out (and docu-

6 Including same sex spouse: paragraph 1 of Schedule 3 to the Marriage (Same Sex Couples) Act 2013.

7 Paragraph 3 of Schedule 4 to the Civil Partnership Act 2004.

8 This is considered further at 2.6.

mented), it will give rise to a very strong presumption that the will represents the testator's intentions (i.e. that the testator knew and approved its contents).[9]

- That exercise will also give the solicitor a further opportunity to assess whether the client has testamentary capacity. It should be borne in mind that it is the testator's capacity when he signs the will which is key, and not his capacity when he previously gave instructions in relation to his will.[10] This is particularly important if a significant amount of time has passed since the meeting at which the client gave instructions and if there is reason to think the client's capacity may have declined in the meantime. The attendance note of the meeting at which the will is executed should therefore also record the solicitor's assessment of the testator's testamentary capacity – something which in practice is all too frequently overlooked by many solicitors, whose attendance note of the meeting at which the will is executed is often no more than one or two lines long.

- The solicitor can also make sure that he brings with him to the meeting – and takes away from the meeting – an engrossment of the will which is printed on suitably durable paper and which is properly bound. This should ensure that the will remains legible even if it is kept in storage for many years – possibly even decades – and that the Probate Registry does not then query whether its various pages do in fact form

9 See e.g. *Gill v Woodall* [2010] EWCA Civ 1430 at [14]-[15].

10 Although the rule in *Parker v Felgate* might be relevant if the testator had testamentary capacity when he gave instructions but his capacity had then declined by the time he executed the will: see 2.3.

part of the same document or ask any questions about the reason for any stapling when the original will is submitted as part of the application for a grant.

One of the main difficulties caused by the pandemic is the inability to arrange face-to-face meetings during which the will can be executed. This means that it will be necessary to find alternative – and generally less satisfactory – ways of addressing those matters.

In many cases it is possible to adopt a creative version of process (a) even during the pandemic. Some very old authorities involving wills executed in slightly unusual circumstances have returned to the spotlight, as they provide helpful illustrations of when a testator is and is not considered as having signed "*in the presence of*" the witnesses as required by section 9. The most relevant examples include *Shires v Glascock*,[11] *Eccleston v Petty*,[12] *Davy and Nicholas v Smith*,[13] *Broderick v Broderick*,[14] *Longford v Eyre*,[15] *Stonehouse v Evelyn*,[16] *Right v Price*,[17] *Casson v Dade*[18] (the now famous case in which Honora Jenkins signed her will in her carriage because she suffered from asthma and her solicitor's office was unusually hot), *Doe d. Wright v Manifold*[19] and *Newton and Thomas v Clarke*.[20]

11 (1687) 2 Salk 688.
12 (1689) 3 Mod 259.
13 (1693) 3 Salk 395.
14 (1713) 1 P Wms 239.
15 (1721) 1 PW 740.
16 (1734) 3 P W 252.
17 (1779) 1 Douglas 241.
18 (1781) 1 Bro CC 99.
19 (1813) 1 M & S 294
20 (1839) 2 Curteis 320.

In general terms, the most important requirement is that there must a clear line of sight between the testator and both witnesses. Provided a clear line of sight exists and can be maintained throughout the process, then it is possible for the three individuals to maintain appropriate distance from one another, and even to be on opposite sides of a glass pane (such as a window or glass door).

Government guidance published on 25th July 2020[21] confirms this and provides:

> *The following scenarios would lead to a properly executed will during the pandemic within the existing law, provided that the will maker and the witnesses each have a clear line of sight:*
>
> - *witnessing through a window or open door of a house or a vehicle*
> - *witnessing from a corridor or adjacent room into a room with the door open*
> - *witnessing outdoors from a short distance, for example in a garden*

Here are some suggested examples of possible solutions:

1. The testator and two witnesses arrange to meet in a driveway or car park. One of them – generally the testator – should bring the will. When the witnesses can see the testator and the will, the testator should sign the will, for example on the bonnet of his car, while both witnesses watch him do so. He should then leave the will on the car bonnet and move away from it and allow the first witness to approach the will and sign

21 https://www.gov.uk/guidance/guidance-on-making-wills-using-video-conferencing (accessed 29th July 2020).

it, while both the testator and the second witness watch him do so. Once the first witness has also signed the will, he too should leave the will on the car bonnet and move away from it and allow the second witness to approach the will and sign it, while both the testator and the first witness watch him do so. The will should then be left on the car bonnet so that the person who will ultimately keep it – usually the testator – can collect it and take it with him.

2. A variation on the above is that the testator could be in his car with the will while the two witnesses are outside the car in a position which allows them both to see the testator sign the will inside the car (e.g. one on either side of the car looking in through the windows). The testator can sign the will inside the car while both witnesses watch him do so, and then pass it to the first witness through the car window, which can be opened only slightly so that the will can be slid through it. The first witness can then sign the will, for example on the car bonnet, while both the testator and the second witness watch him do so. Once again, when the first witness has also signed, he should leave the will on the car bonnet and move away from it and allow the second witness to approach the will and sign it, while both the testator and the first witness watch him do so. The will can then be slid back through the car window to the testator.

3. In some circumstances, it may be possible to follow the rationale of example 2 above by using windows which look into the testator's home – such as an openable window, a see-through front door or French doors which lead onto a garden or patio. The testator can sign the will inside the house while the two witnesses watch him do so through the window. The will can then be slid under or through the window or door to

the witnesses outside. Obviously this will usually only work where the testator's home is on, or comprises, the ground floor. An important point to bear in mind here is that the will should not leave the line of sight of any of the three participants until it has been signed by all. This is to avoid any argument that it – or some of its pages – may have been switched while the document was out of sight. So for example it would be unwise for the testator to sign the will, say, in the living room while the witnesses watch through a window, if in order to then pass the will to the witnesses, the testator will have to walk along a corridor – out of sight of the witnesses – to a front door or openable window.

Another similar example, but which involves process (b) rather than (a) above, is the following:

4. The testator signs the will while alone at home. When the witnesses arrive, the testator passes the will he has already signed through the front door letterbox or slides it under the door. The testator remains inside the house and goes to a window from which he can see the two witnesses outside, and vice versa. When all three can see each other, the testator acknowledges that the signature on the will is his. The two witnesses then each sign the will in turn while both the testator and the other witness watch.

In all of these examples, it is sensible for each of the witnesses to arrive at the meeting already armed with their own pen, and also with a mask or other face covering, and perhaps gloves.

It will also be crucial to document precisely how the will was executed by keeping a detailed, comprehensive and contemporaneous step-by-step account of the process. In controversial cases, such evidence will be helpful in trying to fend off a challenge to the validity of the will by a disappointed beneficiary; however, even in uncontroversial cases, such evidence could be very useful if the Probate Registry were later to query whether the will was validly executed.

If one of the witnesses is the solicitor responsible for also drafting the will, then he should of course take a detailed attendance note of the process – the more detailed, the better – and keep it as part of the will file. It may also be a good idea to make use of the now ubiquitous ability to take video recordings on mobile phones by having one of the three participants, or perhaps a non-participating bystander, film the whole process so that the video recording can then be kept as part of the electronic will file.

In practice many solicitors who know they will not be present or directly involved in the execution process send the client step-by-step instructions as to how the process should be undertaken together with the engrossment. It is interesting to note that there are currently two apparently conflicting first instance authorities on whether this is actually enough for the solicitor to discharge his duty of care, or whether the solicitor should in every case at least offer to attend the client's home to supervise the execution of the will where the client cannot attend the solicitor's office.[22] As a result of this, and in light of the additional difficulties with the execution process caused by the pandemic, it seems prudent for the solicitor to at least offer to, in effect, supervise the execution remotely by video link if he cannot attend in person. The solicitor can talk the client and the two witnesses through the process step by step over the video link, and it should be possible to also record the meeting so that a video recording of the process can then be kept as part of the electronic will file. If this sort of 'live' supervision is not possible, it may be

22 Contrast *Esterhuizen v Allied Dunbar Assurance plc* [1998] 2 FLR 668 and Gray v Richards Butler (a firm) [2000] WTLR 143.

worth arranging for the client to call the solicitor immediately after the execution process is completed and provide a step-by-step account of what happened, so that the solicitor can both make a detailed attendance note of what the client tells him, and give appropriate advice if the process was not completed correctly. If the solicitor was not present and a video recording of the process was made, the client should be asked to send the recording to the solicitor so that, similarly, the solicitor can review it and store it as part of the electronic will file, and if necessary give the client appropriate advice if the process was not completed correctly.

Wherever family members or friends are asked to act as witnesses, it must be remembered that section 15 of the Wills Act 1837 will invalidate any gift made in the will to a witness or to the witness' spouse or civil partner (see 2.6).

3.9 Execution – over a video link

On 25th July 2020 the government published both a press release[23] and guidance[24] addressing the vexed question of whether a will can be validly executed over a video link.

The government has announced that it intends to pass temporary secondary legislation in September 2020 which will make it clear that a will executed over a video link during the pandemic is formally valid. The legislation will apply retrospectively to wills made since 31st January 2020 and is likely to remain in force for 2 years (until 31st January 2022), or possibly less if the pandemic ends sooner.

---

23 https://www.gov.uk/government/news/video-witnessed-wills-to-be-made-legal-during-coronavirus-pandemic (accessed 29th July 2020).

24 https://www.gov.uk/guidance/guidance-on-making-wills-using-video-conferencing (accessed 29th July 2020).

The guidance makes it clear that "*where people can make wills in the conventional way they should continue to do so*". Section 9 of the Wills Act 1837 will not be amended; rather, the government's intention is to make it clear that the requirement imposed by section 9(1)(c) that the testator must sign or acknowledge his signature "*in the presence of*" two witnesses is satisfied even where the two witnesses are present over a video link, rather than physically present in person in the same place.

The guidance indicates that the "*type of video-conferencing or device used is not important, as long as the person making the will and their two witnesses each have a clear line of sight of the writing of the signature*". It is also essential that the witnesses actually witness the writing of the signature in real time: it will not be permissible for the witnesses to watch at a later date a video recording made earlier of the testator signing his will. The guidance expressly encourages the participants to record the video link meeting if possible, pointing out that a recording might help a court in the event of a subsequent challenge.

The following are included in the guidance as examples of the sorts of circumstances in which "*video-witnessing might appropriately be used*":

> *Example 1:*
>
> *the testator (T) is alone and witness one (W1) is physically present with witness two (W2). Together, W1 and W2 are on a two-way live-action video-conferencing link with T*
>
> *Example 2:*
>
> *T, W1 and W2 are all alone in separate locations and are connected by a three-way live-action video-conferencing link.*

Example 3:

T is physically present with W1, and they are connected to W2 by a two-way live-action video-conferencing link.

Example 4:

T is physically present with a person signing the will on their behalf (and at their direction), and connected to W1 and W2 by two or three-way live-action video-conferencing (depending on whether W1 and W2 are in the same or separate locations)

The guidance also contains the following illustration of how the process might work, broken down into five stages:

Stage 1:

- *The person making the will ensures that their two witnesses can see them, each other and their actions.*
- *The will maker or the witnesses should ask for the making of the will to be recorded*
- *The will maker should hold the front page of the will document up to the camera to show the witnesses, and then turn to the page they will be signing and hold this up as well.*
- *By law, the witnesses must see the will-maker (or someone signing at their direction, on their behalf) signing the will. Before signing, the will-maker should ensure that the witnesses can see them actually writing their signature on the will, not just their head and shoulders.*

- *If the witnesses do not know the person making the will they should ask for confirmation of the person's identity - such as a passport or driving licence.*

Stage 2:

- *The witnesses should confirm that they can see, hear (unless they have a hearing impairment), acknowledge and understand their role in witnessing the signing of a legal document. Ideally, they should be physically present with each other but if this is not possible, they must be present at the same time by way of a two or three-way video-link.*

Stage 3:

- *The will document should then be taken to the two witnesses for them to sign, ideally within 24 hours. It must be the same document [...]*

- *A longer period of time between the will-maker and witnesses signing the will may be unavoidable (for example if the document has to be posted) but it should be borne in mind that the longer this process takes the greater the potential for problems to arise.*

- *A will is fully validated only when testators (or someone at their direction) and both witnesses have signed it and either been witnessed signing it or have acknowledged their signature to the testator. This means there is a risk that if the will-maker dies before the full process has taken place the partly completed will is not legally effective.*

Stage 4:

- *The next stage is for the two witnesses to sign the will document – this will normally involve the person who has made the will seeing both the witnesses sign and acknowledge they have seen them sign.*

- *Both parties (the witness and the will maker) must be able to see and understand what is happening.*

- *The witnesses should hold up the will to the will maker to show them that they are signing it and should then sign it (again the will maker should see them writing their names, not just see their heads and shoulders).*

- *Alternatively, the witness should hold up the signed will so that the will maker can clearly see the signature and confirm to the will maker that it is their signature. They may wish to reiterate their intention, for example saying: "this is my signature, intended to give effect to my intention to make this will".*

- *This session should be recorded if possible.*

Stage 5:

- *If the two witnesses are not physically present with each other when they sign then step 4 will need to take place twice, in both cases ensuring that the will maker and the other witness can clearly see and follow what is happening. While it is not a legal requirement for the two witnesses to sign in the presence of each other, it is good practice.*

- *Consideration may be given to the drafting or amending of the attestation clause in a will where video-witnessing is used. The attestation clause is the part of the will that deals with the witnessing of the will makers signature. For video-witnessed wills it may be advisable to mention that virtual witnessing has occurred, along with details of whether a recording is available.*

It is notable that the above appears to be merely an illustration of how the process might work; it remains to be seen quite how prescriptive the legislation will be.[25]

It is also important to note that the guidance expressly indicates that electronic signatures are not allowed – so traditional 'wet' signatures must be used – and that counterpart documents are also not allowed – i.e. the signatures of the testator and of the two witnesses must ultimately all be on one single original document, not two counterparts. The latter requirement is particularly significant, as it means the will is not complete (and therefore is not a valid will) until all three individuals have actually signed the same document. This means that where the original will signed by the testator has to be posted to the witnesses, perhaps successively, there is a risk (which the guidance recognises) that the will will be invalid if the testator

25 For examples of equivalent legislation enacted in other jurisdictions, see:

- Jersey: regulation 4 of the Covid-19 (Signing Of Instruments) (Jersey) Regulations 2020 (https://www.jerseylaw.je/laws/enacted/Pages/RO-050-2020.aspx, accessed 29th July 2020);
- New Zealand: Epidemic Preparedness (Wills Act 2007—Signing and Witnessing of Wills) Immediate Modification Order 2020 (http://www.legislation.govt.nz/regulation/public/2020/0065/latest/whole.html, accessed 29th July 2020); and
- Queensland: Practice Direction 10 of 2020 (https://www.courts.qld.gov.au/about/news/news233/2020/supreme-court-practice-direction-10-of-2020, accessed 29th July 2020).

dies after he has signed the will, but before the two witnesses have also both signed it (even if the two witnesses watched the testator sign it over a video link).

Finally, it must once again be remembered that wherever family members or friends are asked to act as witnesses, section 15 of the Wills Act 1837 will invalidate any gift made in the will to a witness or to the witness' spouse or civil partner (see 2.6).

3.10 Receiving the will back from the client

If the solicitor is present at the execution of the will, he will usually take the original executed will back to the office for safekeeping. If the solicitor is not going to be present, some thought should be given in advance as to how the client will return the original will to the solicitor for safekeeping once it has been executed, e.g. whether the solicitor should include a self-addressed stamped envelope when sending the engrossment which the client can use to return the signed will, or perhaps whether the client or someone on his behalf will be able to take the signed will to the solicitor's office personally.

Solicitors should bear in mind that when they receive a signed will back from the client for safekeeping, they are under a duty to check that the will at least appears on its face to have been properly executed.[26]

Anecdotal evidence suggests that some firms are encouraging clients to contact them once travel restrictions and social distancing measures have been eased in order to review, and possibly re-execute, wills made during the pandemic.

---

26 *Humblestone v Martin Tolhurst Partnership (A Firm)* [2004] EWHC 151 (Ch).

CHAPTER FOUR
PARTICULAR PROBLEMS

4.1 Introduction

Chapter 3 considered in general terms some of the difficulties caused by the Covid-19 pandemic, and some suggestions were made as to how these might be overcome. In this chapter the focus will be on the following particularly problematic cases: the client who is self-isolating or shielding at home; the client who is in a care home; and the client who is in hospital.

4.2 Client who is self-isolating or shielding at home

'Self-isolating' and 'shielding' are two of the new words which have entered everyday parlance as a result of the pandemic (alongside 'social distancing', and of course 'Covid-19' and 'coronavirus' themselves).

In general terms, a client should self-isolate when he suspects he might have been infected by Covid-19. At the time of writing,[1] government guidance indicates that a person should self-isolate if he develops any of the following:

- a high temperature;
- a new, continuous cough;
- a loss of, or change to, your sense of smell or taste.

---

1 29th July 2020. The latest government guidance is available here: https://www.gov.uk/coronavirus

On the other hand, a client should shield if he is "*clinically extremely vulnerable*" to Covid-19, which according to current government guidance means that he is suffering from certain "*medical conditions that, based on what we know about the virus so far, place some people at greatest risk of severe illness from COVID-19.*"[2]

The key question when a client is self-isolating or shielding will be whether he is able to communicate with the solicitor electronically, in particular by email and by video link. If he is, then it should be possible for the solicitor to accept instructions to help the client make a new will by adopting some of the possible solutions outlined in chapter 3.

If a self-isolating client is showing severe Covid-19 symptoms, the solicitor should carefully consider whether the client's testamentary capacity might be impaired. The solicitor should also consider the client's instructions against the background of the circumstances in which the client is self-isolating or shielding, and critically evaluate whether those instructions are controversial or surprising and, if so, whether they should be explored or tested in some detail with the client. Examples might include:

- an elderly client who is otherwise close to his four adult children and who gives instructions for a new will leaving his whole estate to the live-in carer with whom the client has been shielding for the past 6 weeks;

- a client who is self-isolating with one of his adult children and gives instructions for a new will leaving his whole estate to that child, excluding his two other children;

---

2 https://www.gov.uk/government/publications/guidance-on-shielding-and-protecting-extremely-vulnerable-persons-from-covid-19/guidance-on-shielding-and-protecting-extremely-vulnerable-persons-from-covid-19, which also providse a list of the relevant medical conditions (accessed 29th July 2020).

- a client who has been shielding with his wife of 30 years and who gives instructions for a new will leaving his whole estate to a lady he has recently met online.

Furthermore, particular care will have to be taken at any stage which involves any degree of physical proximity between the client and others to ensure that nobody's health is put at risk. Usually, the stage at which this will be most relevant will be execution if this is to take place in person (as to which see 3.8) – although see also 3.9 in relation to the possibility of execution taking place over a video link.

On the other hand, if the client cannot communicate electronically, the situation becomes very difficult. The solicitor will no doubt want to explore some creative ways to overcome the practical difficulties caused by not being able to meet the client face-to-face or over a video link. However, the solicitor must also bear in mind the tension that can exist between wanting to help the client in difficult circumstances and not being able to properly discharge his duty of care because of those circumstances. In very problematic cases, the solicitor should not forget that one of his options is to refuse to accept the client's instructions. Although this is never an attractive option, pressing on with helping a client make a will through a process which is flawed, or at least open to challenge, may ultimately prove to be a greater disservice to the client – as well as a source of trouble for the solicitor – than refusing to accept instructions, particularly where the risk of challenge is high (e.g. because of the client's already fraught family dynamics).

4.3 Client in a care home

Tragically, care homes appear to have been affected particularly badly by the pandemic. As a result, any interaction with a client who is in a care home is likely to be challenging for as long as a risk of infection exists.

Once again, the key question will be whether the client is able to communicate electronically with the solicitor from the care home, primarily by email and by video link.

If he is, then it might be possible for a new will to be made. The solicitor should generally be particularly alert in relation to assessing the client's testamentary capacity, which can be harder to do if the majority of the interaction with the client is virtual. The 'golden rule' should be followed if at all possible.[3] It will usually also be a good idea to liaise with the care home at the outset of the process as to how the will can be executed (if at all). Many care homes prohibit staff from acting as witnesses for documents signed by their residents. It may or may not be possible to find two other capacitous[4] residents of the home to act as witnesses. All of this can cause real difficulties if the care home is itself, in effect, in lockdown to protect its residents from the risk of a Covid-19 outbreak. In these cases it may be possible for the will to be executed over a video link if one is available (see 3.9).

3 See 2.3.

4 The witnesses need to have sufficient mental capacity to understand that they are witnessing a will: see e.g. *Hudson v Parker* (1844) 1 RobEcc 14 which interpreted "presence" in section 9 of the Wills Act 1837 as requiring the witnesses to be "*mentally, as well as bodily, present*".

On the other hand, if the client cannot communicate electronically from the care home, then the situation will be very difficult indeed. The solicitor can of course try to think of and explore creative solutions if possible, but it may well be that he will ultimately have little choice but to refuse to accept the client's instructions.

4.4 Client in hospital

Similarly to care homes, hospitals are another place in which the consequences of a Covid-19 outbreak are potentially catastrophic. Therefore, in general, interaction with a client who is in hospital is also likely to be difficult.

The solicitor will of course need to carefully assess the particular circumstances. Taking will instructions from a 38-year-old client who is temporarily in hospital recuperating from a broken ankle is likely to be much less problematic than doing so for an 82-year-old client who has been diagnosed with Covid-19 and is in ICU on a ventilator.

Once again, the key question will be whether the client is able to communicate electronically from hospital, primarily by email and by video link. If he is, then it may well be possible for the solicitor to help. However, if he is not, if the circumstances are such that the solicitor cannot confidently take the client's instructions and/or if it will not be possible for the new will to be validly executed at the end of the process, then the solicitor should seriously consider refusing to accept instructions.

MORE BOOKS BY LAW BRIEF PUBLISHING

A selection of our other titles available now:-

'Covid-19, Homeworking and the Law – The Essential Guide to Employment and GDPR Issues' by Forbes Solicitors
'Covid-19, Force Majeure and Frustration of Contracts – The Essential Guide' by Keith Markham
'Covid-19 and Criminal Law – The Essential Guide' by Ramya Nagesh
'Covid-19 and Family Law in England and Wales – The Essential Guide' by Safda Mahmood
'Covid-19 and the Implications for Planning Law – The Essential Guide' by Bob Mc Geady & Meyric Lewis
'Covid-19, Residential Property, Equity Release and Enfranchisement – The Essential Guide' by Paul Sams and Louise Uphill
'Covid-19, Brexit and the Law of Commercial Leases – The Essential Guide' by Mark Shelton
'Covid-19 and the Law Relating to Food in the UK and Republic of Ireland – The Essential Guide' by Ian Thomas
'A Practical Guide to the General Data Protection Regulation (GDPR) – 2nd Edition' by Keith Markham
'Ellis on Credit Hire – Sixth Edition' by Aidan Ellis & Tim Kevan
'A Practical Guide to Working with Litigants in Person and McKenzie Friends in Family Cases' by Stuart Barlow
'Protecting Unregistered Brands: A Practical Guide to the Law of Passing Off' by Lorna Brazell
'A Practical Guide to Secondary Liability and Joint Enterprise Post-Jogee' by Joanne Cecil & James Mehigan

'A Practical Guide to the Pre-Action RTA Claims Protocol for Personal Injury Lawyers' by Antonia Ford
'A Practical Guide to Neighbour Disputes and the Law' by Alexander Walsh
'A Practical Guide to Forfeiture of Leases' by Mark Shelton
'A Practical Guide to Coercive Control for Legal Practitioners and Victims' by Rachel Horman
'A Practical Guide to Rights Over Airspace and Subsoil' by Daniel Gatty
'Tackling Disclosure in the Criminal Courts – A Practitioner's Guide' by Narita Bahra QC & Don Ramble
'A Practical Guide to the Law of Driverless Cars – Second Edition' by Alex Glassbrook, Emma Northey & Scarlett Milligan
'A Practical Guide to TOLATA Claims' by Greg Williams
'Artificial Intelligence – The Practical Legal Issues' by John Buyers
'A Practical Guide to the Law of Prescription in Scotland' by Andrew Foyle
'A Practical Guide to the Construction and Rectification of Wills and Trust Instruments' by Edward Hewitt
'A Practical Guide to the Law of Bullying and Harassment in the Workplace' by Philip Hyland
'How to Be a Freelance Solicitor: A Practical Guide to the SRA-Regulated Freelance Solicitor Model' by Paul Bennett
'A Practical Guide to Prison Injury Claims' by Malcolm Johnson
'A Practical Guide to the Small Claims Track' by Dominic Bright
'A Practical Guide to Advising Clients at the Police Station' by Colin Stephen McKeown-Beaumont
'A Practical Guide to Antisocial Behaviour Injunctions' by Iain Wightwick
'Practical Mediation: A Guide for Mediators, Advocates, Advisers, Lawyers, and Students in Civil, Commercial, Business, Property, Workplace, and Employment Cases' by Jonathan Dingle with John Sephton
'The Mini-Pupillage Workbook' by David Boyle

‘A Practical Guide to Crofting Law’ by Brian Inkster
‘A Practical Guide to Spousal Maintenance’ by Liz Cowell
‘A Practical Guide to the Law of Domain Names and Cybersquatting’ by Andrew Clemson
‘A Practical Guide to the Law of Gender Pay Gap Reporting’ by Harini Iyengar
‘A Practical Guide to the Rights of Grandparents in Children Proceedings’ by Stuart Barlow
‘NHS Whistleblowing and the Law’ by Joseph England
‘Employment Law and the Gig Economy’ by Nigel Mackay & Annie Powell
‘A Practical Guide to Noise Induced Hearing Loss (NIHL) Claims’ by Andrew Mckie, Ian Skeate, Gareth McAloon
‘An Introduction to Beauty Negligence Claims – A Practical Guide for the Personal Injury Practitioner’ by Greg Almond
‘Intercompany Agreements for Transfer Pricing Compliance’ by Paul Sutton
‘Zen and the Art of Mediation’ by Martin Plowman
‘A Practical Guide to the SRA Principles, Individual and Law Firm Codes of Conduct 2019 – What Every Law Firm Needs to Know’ by Paul Bennett
‘A Practical Guide to Adoption for Family Lawyers’ by Graham Pegg
‘A Practical Guide to Industrial Disease Claims’ by Andrew Mckie & Ian Skeate
‘A Practical Guide to Redundancy’ by Philip Hyland
‘A Practical Guide to Vicarious Liability’ by Mariel Irvine
‘A Practical Guide to Applications for Landlord’s Consent and Variation of Leases’ by Mark Shelton
‘A Practical Guide to Relief from Sanctions Post-Mitchell and Denton’ by Peter Causton
‘A Practical Guide to Equity Release for Advisors’ by Paul Sams
‘A Practical Guide to Unlawful Eviction and Harassment’ by Stephanie Lovegrove
‘A Practical Guide to the Law Relating to Food’ by Ian Thomas

'A Practical Guide to Financial Services Claims' by Chris Hegarty
'The Law of Houses in Multiple Occupation: A Practical Guide to HMO Proceedings' by Julian Hunt
'A Practical Guide to Unlawful Eviction and Harassment' by Stephanie Lovegrove
'A Practical Guide to Solicitor and Client Costs' by Robin Dunne
'Occupiers, Highways and Defective Premises Claims: A Practical Guide Post-Jackson – 2nd Edition' by Andrew Mckie
'A Practical Guide to Financial Ombudsman Service Claims' by Adam Temple & Robert Scrivenor
'A Practical Guide to Advising Schools on Employment Law' by Jonathan Holden
'A Practical Guide to Running Housing Disrepair and Cavity Wall Claims: 2nd Edition' by Andrew Mckie & Ian Skeate
'A Practical Guide to Holiday Sickness Claims – 2nd Edition' by Andrew Mckie & Ian Skeate
'Arguments and Tactics for Personal Injury and Clinical Negligence Claims' by Dorian Williams
'A Practical Guide to QOCS and Fundamental Dishonesty' by James Bentley
'A Practical Guide to Drone Law' by Rufus Ballaster, Andrew Firman, Eleanor Clot
'A Practical Guide to Compliance for Personal Injury Firms Working With Claims Management Companies' by Paul Bennett
'A Practical Guide to the Landlord and Tenant Act 1954: Commercial Tenancies' by Richard Hayes & David Sawtell
'A Practical Guide to Dog Law for Owners and Others' by Andrea Pitt
'RTA Allegations of Fraud in a Post-Jackson Era: The Handbook – 2nd Edition' by Andrew Mckie
'RTA Personal Injury Claims: A Practical Guide Post-Jackson' by Andrew Mckie
'On Experts: CPR35 for Lawyers and Experts' by David Boyle
'An Introduction to Personal Injury Law' by David Boyle

'A Practical Guide to Chronic Pain Claims' by Pankaj Madan
'A Practical Guide to Claims Arising from Fatal Accidents' by James Patience
'A Practical Guide to Subtle Brain Injury Claims' by Pankaj Madan

These books and more are available to order online direct from the publisher at www.lawbriefpublishing.com, where you can also read free sample chapters. For any queries, contact us on 0844 587 2383 or mail@lawbriefpublishing.com.

Our books are also usually in stock at www.amazon.co.uk with free next day delivery for Prime members, and at good legal bookshops such as Wildy & Sons.

We are regularly launching new books in our series of practical day-to-day practitioners' guides. Visit our website and join our free newsletter to be kept informed and to receive special offers, free chapters, etc.

You can also follow us on Twitter at www.twitter.com/lawbriefpub.

www.ingramcontent.com/pod-product-compliance
Ingram Content Group UK Ltd.
Pitfield, Milton Keynes, MK11 3LW, UK
UKHW020152290926
15471UKWH00004B/820

Edward Hewitt is a barrister at 5 Stone Buildings in Lincoln's Inn. He has a private client practice with a particular emphasis on inheritance and trust disputes. He is frequently asked to advise and represent clients in cases involving challenges to the validity of wills and codicils, and was counsel in recent leading probate cases including James v James and *Kunicki v Hayward.*